THE AYODHYA VERDICT: JUSTICE DONE OR JUSTICE DENIED?

VOLUME 1, ISSUE 4 OF BRILLOPEDIA

ANINDO CHATTERJEE

ISBN 979-888530609-6

Contents

Preface   *v*

Author   *vii*

Publication   *ix*

1. Abstract   1

2. Introduction   3

3. Aim   4

4. History Of Ayodhya   5

5. Importance Of This Much Celebrated City   6

6. History Of Babri Masjid   8

7. The Phase Before Independence   10

8. Post-independence Scenario   11

9. Direct Connection With The Recent Case   12

10. Real Trouble Begins   13

11. After Wreckage Scenario   14

12. The Puzzling Judgement   15

13. The Final Frontier   16

14. High Court Of Allahabad's Decision- How Justifiable?   17

15. Significance Of Lord Ram In Sanatan Dharma Or Hindusim   18

16. Authenticity Of Uttara Kanda   20

17. Significance Of Shri Ram In The Indian Tradition   21

18. Stakes On The Muslim Side   22

19. Stakes On The Hindu Side   23

20. Historical View Of Jurisprudence   24

21. Sociological School Of Jurisprudence   26

22. Which Of The Two To Choose Regarding This Verdict Or A   28
    Combination?

23. Analysis Of The Historic Ayodhya Verdict   30

24. Conclusion   33

Preface

"Start writing, no matter what. The water does not flow until the faucet is turned on".

-Louis L'Amour

Hundreds of students and professors are contributing their work to Brillopedia, we are here to provide ample information about Law and Contemporary issues. Our aim is to provide a platform for today's generation to express their views and ideas on law and contemporary law.

Author

Publication

This research paper is published in volume 1, issue 4 of Brillopedia

CHAPTER ONE

Abstract

"Faith is a matter of Individual belief. Value of a secular constitution lies in mutual deference"

-Five judges' bench

In the history of India, there have been a number of landmark judgments from the highest court but only a few were as sensitive and complex as the Ayodhya verdict that was pronounced by the highest court on 9th November, 2019, settling once and for all what had been a prolonged dispute. This particular paper is not merely based on the final judgement but to also the premise building to that point. The paper begins with giving the introduction which gives a small yet very intriguing facts of case while also raising some questions on high court's judgement made in the year of 2010, mentioning that the topic is sourced from a religious, historical and other aspects. The aim highlights the main focus of this particular paper and the methodology focuses on how the conclusion that was preferred arrived at. Then before moving on to the case,we will also dive into history of the great city of Ayodhya and the importance it has held for years in for India's different faiths. By this we can say that history plays a key role in this entire dispute's analysis. A lot for the historical side of affairs but the problem is that it's not the only perspective as we then move to the religious aspects in this particular case in the sense,people already have a glance at the life as according to the sacred text related to main party in this case Shree Ram (Ram Lalla), what are the specialities and qualities that made Lord Ram so significant which makes him so revered among the masses. We also discuss few of the occasions related to Lord Ram that imprints its impact on almost every life. We then discuss the stakes at both sides that help us realise how much importance it holds to both sides involved (not parties) because there are numerous parties but only two sides when seen ona wider scale. Finally, we move on to the jurisprudential aspect regarding this case where we discuss two approaches the historical approach and sociological approach and how there is no approach of monocentric nature rather a mix of two before getting to the analysis and conclusion. Main focus of the analysis is on the impacts those decisions have in the judgement upon both parties as well as reasoning that is possible behind it, at last we conclude where does this judgement stand in terms of doing proper justice with to both the parties.

CHAPTER TWO

Introduction

Ayodhya the holy land of Shri Ram, the land almost every interested Indian wants to visit once before respectfully accepting the death-bed this was a dispute that shook the entirety of India by the sheer duration and possible religious riots brimming around the corner in that particular region. India is a secular country by the very endowments of the constitution it inherited from its forefathers but instances exists where the Supreme courtitself has with its competence upheld what was called a balanced judgement by him and one of those judgements was Ayodhya Verdict. Although, an argument can be raised by some why the land didn't come in possession of Sunni Wakf Board because they say the Babri Masjid was demolished by some assailants, while Ram Lalla Vrajman (the Hindu God was considered a juristic person) party made an argument stating no offering was made to Namaz by the Muslims but there was evidence of Hindus offering worshipsat different sites in the area that was disputed which was around 2.44 acre. The Allahabad High court's decisionabout this matter was that this land was to be made three parts of, without any proper evidences of ownership and it seemed as if the particular decision that has been made was purely to serve a purpose of preventing any riots. While on surface it seems that the HC judgement was a wise decision to prevent unrest but by a close look the problems lie bare in that said judgement. Let us further look into this case but not only a legal glance but also historical, social, religious, jurisprudentialglance (in no specified order) that will help us deeply correlate and understand the case at nota superficiallevel.

CHAPTER THREE

Aim

To decode the long judgement by the honourable court and look into the details of this case from the historical aspect to the jurisprudential aspect and hence arriving at a conclusion regarding the effectiveness of this crucial judgement.

Methodology

If we dive into the historical and religious roots that the judgment was based upon and reading, comprehending the judgement given by the honourable court and analysing the jurisprudential aspect and hence arriving at an effective at a conclusion that does justice to this long-drawn dispute.

CHAPTER FOUR

History of Ayodhya

Ayodhya is an old city of India, that holds an appreciated spot in the confidence of Hindus, Jains, Buddhists, and Muslims. The Ramayana, a Hindu work of art, depicts the magnificence of the city, the excellencies of the rulers, and the faithfulness and thriving individuals. Hindus generally accept that Ayodhya had been the origination of Lord Ram, at Ram Janmabhoomi, the place where exists the destroyed Babri Mosque. With the ascent of an empire named Gupta Empire (320 to 550 AD), Hinduism again rose in Ayodhya, entering a brilliant age. The Gupta Empire covered northern India, Afghanistan, Bangladesh, and Tibet.

For Jainism, Ayodhya is a holy spot on the grounds that Jain's sacred text relates that five Tirthankars, including the originator of Jainism and the main Tirthankar, ShriRishabhDev, lived in Ayodhya. For Buddhists, Ayodhya holds an uncommon spot as a middle for Buddhism during the Mauryan Empire (322–185 B.C.E.). Ashoka the Great had been the extraordinary advertiser of Buddhism, extending the Mauryan Empire to cover virtually all of the region of present-day India. At the pinnacle of his realm building, Ashoka denied war and changed over to Buddhism, proclaiming Buddhism as the domain's religion and setting up Buddhist sanctuaries all through. Ayodhya became one of the focuses of Buddhism during his rule.[1]

[1]Newworldencyclopedia.org. 2021. *Ayodhya - New World Encyclopedia.* [online] Available at: <https://www.newworldencyclopedia.org/entry/Ayodhya> [Accessed 9 October 2021].

CHAPTER FIVE

Importance of this much celebrated city

Ayodhya additionally filled in as the origin of five Tirthankars, including the primary Shri Rishabh Dev, Tirthankar of Jainism, known as the founder of the respected religion jainism. The city shows its significance in the set of experiences and Buddhism legacy in India, with a few Buddhist sanctuaries, landmarks, and focuses of getting the hang of having been built at this place during the age of the Mauryan Empire and Dynasty of The Gupta. Ayodhya arrived at the pinnacle of its brilliant age during the rule from the Guptas over India. BhagwanSwaminarayan, the organizer of the Swaminarayan faction of Hinduism, lived here during his youth years. BhagwanSwaminarayan began his seven-year venture across India as Neelkanth in Ayodhya. Tulsidas started to compose his popular Ramayana sonnet Shri Ramacharitamanas in Ayodhya in 1574 AD. A few Tamil Alwar makes reference to the city of Ayodhya. Ayodhya had been the origination of Bhahubalee, Brahmee, Sundaree, King Dasarathaa, AcharyPadaliptasurisvarjee, King Harishchandr, Shri Ram, Achalbhraata, and the 10th Gandharaa of Mahaveer Swami. The Atharv Veda referredAyodhya "the city worked by divine beings and being almost as prosperous as heaven itself." Ayodhyawas the survivor of plunder and termination during the Ghaznavi strikes and Ghori intrusions. Some Hindu sanctuaries had been plundered and annihilated. Some accept that the BabriMasjeedhad been built on the remaining parts of a sanctuary, however that guarantee stays questionable. With some Muslim rulers set up on all sides of the city under Mohammad Ghori, The City lost its key and monetary significance to the city of Lucknow and Kanpur.

As indicated by a 11th century Korean narrative the SamgookYusa, the spouse of King Sooro that was from old Korean realm of

Geoomgwan,Gayaaprincess who went by a vessel from a distant land known asAyuta to the region of Korea in 48 AD. The normal point of view has been that the narratives of Korea alluded to Ayodhya, yet a few researchers accept that the unfamiliar land that maybe the city of Ayutthaya of the country Thailand. The Koreans are familiar with the princess as Hio Hwang-alright, the principal sovereign of Geoomgwan Gayaa thought about a precursor by a few Korean heredities.

CHAPTER SIX

History of Babri Masjid

Babri Masjeed, even called the Babari Mosque or Babur Mosque, previously Masjid-I Janmasthan, is a masjeed in Ayodhya, the state of Uttar Pradesh, India. As stipulated by etchingsright there, it is believed that it was inherent in the year nine thirty five(935) of the Islamic schedule (September 1528–September 1529) by MīrBāqī, potentially a particular bey that served the Mughal sovereign Bābur. In conjunction that was within panipat and shambal mosque, from the three masjeeds said to have been created in sixteenth century upon Bābur's orders.Beg or Bey and BEGOM. Beg is a Turkish title signifying "chief or lord" later "crown prince," identical to the Arabic-Persian amīr. The female type of bey is begom (in Mughal India begam) from Turkish begim "woman, princess."[1]The Babarimasjeedwas obliterated in 1992 in the midst of numerous years of pressure regarding the site among Hindus and Muslims. The mosque was built in a style created under the fleeting Lodhī tradition that went before the Mughals: little with a solitary path plan of three domed inlets along with the mass of the qiblah. The passage of the centeralcove—a pīshṭāq underscoring the structure's quality and significance—was impressively at a height more than the ones present on side alcove.

The area that belongs to the mosques was a wellspring of conflict among Muslims and Hindus, the last attesting that it was based on janmabhoomi of Ram,this site is the one they accept to be the origination of the Hindu divinity Rama. The originally recorded occurrence of contention on places in between strict networks was in the year of 1853,this was during a period of socio-political change all through India. In direct British guideline or British raj over the Indian subcontinent, separate spaces that belonged to this particular site was set up for the Hindus and Muslims. In the year of 1949, after India was divided and became free, pictures of lord Rama were made present in the mosque. The site was deferred into twoparts; however, the pictures were not eliminated.[2]

Case History

Before we dive in legalities of the matter it is very important to completely understand the historical element that spurred this historical long drawn dispute.

[1]Iranicaonline.org. 2021. *Welcome to Encyclopaedia Iranica.* [online] Available at: <https://iranicaonline.org/articles/beg-pers> [Accessed 9 October 2021].

[2]Encyclopedia Britannica. 2021. *Babri Masjid | History, Architecture, & Facts.* [online] Available at: <https://www.britannica.com/place/Babri-Masjid> [Accessed 9 October 2021].

CHAPTER SEVEN

The phase before Independence

The initially recorded legitimate history in Ayodhya issue traces all the way back to 1858. A FIR was recorded on November 30, 1858, by one Mohd. Salim against a gathering of Nihang Sikhs who had introduced their nishan and stated "Ram" inside the Babri mosque. They likewise performed havan and puja. Sheetal Dubey, the thanedar (the station house office of yesteryear) of Avadh, in his report on December 1, 1858, checked the protest and surprisingly said that a chabutra (stage) has been built by the Sikhs. This turned into the a primary proof of the fact that Hindus were available in the external patio and inside the internal yard. The legalconflict started in 1885, when Mahanth Raghubar Das recorded a suit (No. 61/280) against Secretary of State for India in Council in the common court of Faizabad. In his suit, Das guaranteed that he was a mahanth and was situated at the chabutra in the external yard and ought to be allowed to develop a sanctuary there. The suit was hence dismissed. In 1886, a Civil Appeal (No. 27) was documented against the 1885 judgment. Region Judge of Faizabad, FER Chamier, chose to visit the spot prior to passing the said order. He later, to the disappointment of the appealing party dismissed the appeal. A second Civil Appeal (No. 122) was documented against this second dismissal, which was once again dismissed by the court of the Judicial Commissioner. For the following 63 years, no lawful advancement in situation. In 1934, an uproar occurred in Ayodhya and Hindus destroyed a part of the design of the contested site. The part was remade into brick and mortar by the Britishers.

CHAPTER EIGHT

Post-Independence scenario

On the mediating evening of December's 22nd and 23rd of 1949, statues of God were found inside the masjeed's focal dome. Then, at that point, Faizabad DM KK Nayar on December 23 morning reiterated UttarPradesh CM Govind Ballabh Pant about a gathering of Hindus entering the site when abandoned and setting the statue of God. A FIR was documented for that situation and the entryways were locked that very day. On December 29, the city magistrate passed a written order under Section 145 of the Criminal procedural code that made sure that all the property is attached and selected, the Nagar Mahapalika"president PriyaDutt Ram" as a collector of the particular property. After seven days, on January 5, of the year 1950, PriyaDutt Ram accepted responsibility as the collector.

On 16th January 1950, Gopaal Singh Visharadd of HinduMahaaSabha turned into the first individual to document a much-anticipated case in quite a while for the situation. GopalVisharad documented a seething case against Muslims that were 5 in number, the government of the state, and also the DM of Faizabad appealing for the option to implore and lead Puja in the inward patio. Around the same time, the common adjudicator passed a request for order and permitted the puja. On May 25, the back-to-back suit was recorded by PramahansRamchandr Das against Zahur Ahmed and others and this wasalmost alike to the primary suit. After nine years, on December 17 of the year 1959, NirmohiAkhaada recorded the triplet completion suit to assume dominion over the administration from the recipient.

Direct connection with the recent case

After two years, on December 18 of the year 1961, Sunni Central Wakf Board alongside that load of respondents named in the prior suits, documented the quartet completion suit in Civil Judge's court, Faizabad, asking for the expulsion of God idols and giving over the ownership of mosque. On March 20, 1963, Court made a decision that whole Hindoo people group can't be addressed by so limited people. It requested regarding a public notification to implead Hindu MahaSabha, AryaSamaaj, and Sanaatan DharmaSabha as litigants to address the Hindu people group.

On July 1 of the year 1989, the quintet of suits was recorded by previous High court of Allahabad's Judge DeokiiNandanAgarwal as the "next companion" of Ram LallaVrajmaan (the god, considered a minor legitimate individual) under the watchful eye of the Faizabad's civil judge. It asked that the entire site be given over to Ram Lala for the development of another sanctuary. In 1989, Shia Wakf Board likewise recorded a suit and turned into a litigant for thisvery case.

CHAPTER TEN

Real Trouble begins

On January 25 of the year1986, UmeshChandrPandey, a lawyer, recorded an application with Munsif Magistrate, Faizabad, supplicating that the locks ought to be opened and people were allowed to have darshn of the god idols which was found inside. The Munsif judge dismissed the application saying documents identified with the matter are under the watchful eye of the high court. Pandey pursued the request in the Faizabad area court on January 31, 1986. On February 1, both DM and SP of Faizabad conceded in the court about not being any issue in keeping up with harmony in case locks are unbolted. Court asked for the kick-off of the locks and it was unbolted around that time. That moment was considered defining in the Ayodhya issue which adjusted India's political direction. After the locks were unfastened, the Muslim chiefs met in Lucknow on February 6 and a Babri Masjid Action Committee was framed with Zafaryab Jilani as the convenor. On July 12, 1989, High court in Allahabad passed an order moving every one of the suits to the High court's three judged bench. On October 7 and 10, 1991, BJP got the premises in question alongside some abutting region (complete 2.77 sections of land) to foster it for the travel industry reason under the land acquisition Act. This procurement was challenged by Muslims through six writ petitions. The procurement was struck down by high court in 11th of December . On the date of 6th December 1992, this mosque was illegally annihilated notwithstanding interim orders passed by high court and supreme court, and 49 FIRs were filed against a few groups, including some BJP leaders, in the destruction case.

CHAPTER ELEVEN

After wreckage scenario

On December 21, 1992, Hari Shankar Jain recorded a request in the Lucknow seat of the Allahabad High Court that his cardinal right in order to revere Lord Ram. On January 1, 1993, high court made it so that each Hindu has the option to revere at the spot accepted to be the origination of Lord Ram. Nonetheless, detecting further difficulty, the union government on January 7, 1993, got an ordinance passed — the Acquisition of Central Area at Ayodhya — gaining 67 number of sections of land of land, including the contested site along with the surrounding regions. Likewise, the union government requested supreme court to decide if there was a Mandir before the development of the Babri mosque. Following the acquisition by the public authority, Mohd. Ismail Farooqi documented petition in Supreme Court challenging it. The SC established a five-judge seat to hear the petition. On October 24, 1994, Supreme court held that the procurement was legitimate. Thirteen years of high court in Allahabad took the case in March 2002, a case hearing started for the title suit of the Ayodhyacase. In July 2003, the Allahabad High Court requested unearthing at the contested site. "The Archaeological Survey of India" (ASI) did the unearthing and presented its report on August 22, 2003. In its report, ASI said that there was a gigantic design underneath the contested construction and there were objects of Hindu faith.

CHAPTER TWELVE

The puzzling judgement

On 30th September, 2010, the threejudged seat of Justice Dharamvir Sharma, Justice Sudheer Agarwal and Justice SU Khaan of high court in Allahabad gave its decision in the suit of title. It separated the land in contention into three sections, distributing one part respectively to Ram Lala, NirmohiAkhada, and Sunni Waqf Board. Every one of the involved parties — Ram LallaVirajman, Sunni Wakf Board, and NirmohiAkhaada — pursued in the highest court that is Supreme courtCourt against the Allahabad high court judgment. On May 9 of the year 2011, a seat of Justices AftaabAlam and RM Lodhha, conceding a cluster of requests from both side of associations, withheld the 2010 judgment of the Lucknow Bench of high court in Allahabad and guided the involved parties to keep up with the norm at the site.

CHAPTER THIRTEEN

The final frontier

On January eighth of thisyear(2020 in this context), the SC put forth a 5judged seat to hear thesuit of title in Ayodhya. After two days, his honor UU Lalit removed himself from the five-judge seat. In February this year itself, Chief Justice of India RanjanGogoii shaped a five-judge seat under him, alongside his honor Ashok Bhooshan, his honorNazir, his honorBobde, and hishonorChandrachud. The seat proposed a court-observed mediation an alternate form of redressal of dispute, Former SC Judge his honor FM Kalifullaa, Sri Ravii Shankar, and senior lawyer SreeramPanchoo were in the constitutedmediation board. The mediation started on the thirteenth March at Faizabad's Awadh University. 7 rounds of conversation occurred however it didn't bear any results. On second August, the court chose to begin ordinary hearings from sixth August. The highest court had heard the case routinely for forty days and during the recent 11 days, 1 additional hour was given for parties to finish their contentions. The contentions from all sides for the situation were finished on 16th October and the judgment was set for later.[1]

[1]Anshuman, K., 2021. *Ayodhya case: A brief history of India's longest running property dispute.* [online] The Economic Times. Available at: <https://economictimes.indiatimes.com/news/politics-and-nation/ ayodhya-case-a-brief-history-of-indias-longest-running-property-dispute/ articleshow/71988076.cms?from=mdr> [Accessed 9 October 2021].

CHAPTER FOURTEEN

High court of Allahabad's decision- how justifiable?

With so much going it is perhaps easy to lose track of what significant is happening but we have not lost track of Allahabad high court three judged bench's decision that divided the disputed land into three parts.

Before moving, it's required to analyse the Allahabad court's judgement that transpired and took a controversial turn, without going much into judgment merits it still comes across as a strange judgement because this court itself in 2003 had requested unearthing of the site by ASI and there were indications that were clearly of Lord Ram temple way before the structure of the Babri Masjid that was funded by the Mughal king Babur. Hence clearly showing a demolition of the original Ram Mandir by the Mughal king Babur before Babri Masjid was even constructed on the site. The claim of someonewhodestroyed cannot be better compared of an original holder and original holder in this case clearly appears to be the Hindu community. Therefore the land that was under dispute was divided land into three might seem outlandish despite the historical evidences present. Yes, it can be contented that it may be done to dissolve communal pressure but it would not change original ownership of the land and the title of the land cannot be altered of the disputed land just due to the fear of communal riots, for sure there might be better alternative but the Allahabad court's Lucknow seat chose the safest option lacking any real conviction.

CHAPTER FIFTEEN

Significance of Lord Ram in Sanatan Dharma or Hindusim

Shree Ram or Ramchandra is the seventh incarnation of Lord Vishnu, the supreme man with honor and righteousness or the Maryada Purshottam. Lord Ram is the epitome of the qualities that a man should possess or aim to possess. Endless valour, strength and infinite talent for archery were only a few of the qualities that were honed by Shree Ramchandra. His life is full of challenges and he is also revered as a man who shows and maintains his best of qualities even in most of adverse of situations. His wife Sita is his beloved one and he is her ideal husband. But everything does not go well as the fairy tales about a kingand queen who lived happily thereafter. His second wife and mother of his beloved brother Bharat, Kaikeyi demands from King Dashrath the father of Shri Ram and king of Ayodhya that he must comply with one thing as demanded by her so then due to that one wish she asks Dashrath the exile of his eldest son Ram to forests for 14 years so that her son (Bharath) could become the king of Ayodhya. Bereaved and heartbroken King Dashrath reluctantly asks his son Ram of the same, and Ram being the ideal son he is at once agrees to abide by his father's words and leave the kingdom along with Sita and younger brother Lakshmana. This unbearable pain of separation from his most beloved elder son Ram breaks King Dashrath and he soon leaves the world to the heavenly abode. Shri Ram while in exile for fourteen years undertakes many adventures but the most grievous being the kidnapping of his beloved wife Sita. It so happens that Mata Sita spots a golden deer and asks Shri Ram to bring it for her actually that deer was nobody else but a trap from the demon king Raavan to lure away Shri Ram and Lakshmana away from Sita and kidnap her. But before leaving for the hunt the younger brother Lakshmana with his powers drew a "Lakshman Rekha" or a safety line that nobody else would be able to cause any harm to Mata Sita by entering into the premises of the hut they were residing in. But the demon king Raavan had other plans, he disguised himself as a sage and asked for alms from Sita but Sita at first hesitantly denied but at some grave insistence from the old sage she stepped outside and was abducted by Raavan who assumed his true form. Long story short after showing great valour, courage and with the help of his great devotees like Lord Hanuman, Sugriva, his brother Lakshmana, Shri Ram finally slaid Raavan and reunited with Sita. But if you are thinking that wow now that is a happy ending you are wrong because even after returning from exile of 14 years, Shri Ram's life was not in any way happier. Despite becoming the king, some naysayers said that Mata Sita should not be the queen since she was abducted by the demon king. Mata Sita gave the Agni Pariksha or the fire test and came out unscathed thus proving he one directional devotion to Shri Ram and both lived and ruled happily ever after. But this is one version of the story another is the UttarKaand.

As per the Uttara Kanda, the story proceeds with Rama actually holding onto doubts about his better half's ethicalness during her bondage with Ravana. Rama along these lines banishes Sita to live with the sage Valmiki, and it is there that she bears him twin children, Kusa and Lava. Ultimately, the children return to Ayodhya where Rama perceives his posterity and, in an attack of regret, reviews the heavily wronged Sita. In the Ramayana everybody lives cheerfully ever after now, however, in the Uttara Kanda, the story isn't exactly wrapped up. As yet declaring her blamelessness, Sita currently swears her ethicalness on the actual earth which then, at that point quickly swallows her by opening underneath her feet. Rama, presently considerably more troubled, pledge to follow his significant other to paradise, yet Time appears to him in the pretence of an austere and calls for him to remain and satisfy his obligation on the planet. All things considered, Rama swims into the waterway Sarayu and from that point is invited into paradise by Brahma.[1]

[1]World History Encyclopedia. 2021. *Rama.* [online] Available at: <https://www.worldhistory.org/Rama/> [Accessed 9 October 2021].

Authenticity of Uttara Kanda

Several questions are raised about authenticity of Uttara Kanda, while some consider it a part of Ramayana others consider this as latter edition to the Ramayana book saying it was written by Valmiki. There are several reasons to think that lack of veracity of the Uttara Kanda, firstly it has an inconsistent writing style, secondly there are issues in Uttara Kanda which harm the reputation of Shree Ram such as asking his wife to leave just because some subjects doubt her, thirdly in all Sanatani or hindupuranic texts it is a process of writing the falashruti or the result of reading the sacred text at the end but not in the middle and it was indeed added at the end of Yuddha Kanda thus indicating that, it was meant to be the end of the sacred texts of Ramayana by sage Valmiki and hence any further additions were frivolous in sense they were not added in ways by the original Author that is sage Valmiki.

Significance of Shri Ram in the Indian tradition

Raam Navami is a spring Hindu celebration that commends the birthday of the Bharatiya God, Lord Rama. He is especially essential to the Vaishnavism custom of Hinduism as the seventh embodiment of God Vishnu the operator of the universe. The celebration commends the descension of Vishnu as Shri Ram embodiment, through his introduction to the world to King Dasharatha and Queen Kausalya in Ayodhya.

The commemoration of a part of the spring Navratri and falls on the 10th day in the bright portion of calendar month of Chaitra. Raam Navamiis government leave day in India. The meaning of the celebration demonstrates the triumph of virtuous over the sinful based on the Dharm to beat the Adharm.

Raam Navami festivity begins with offering jal (water) early morning to the God Sun (a god) to get endowments from him. Individuals likewise accept that God Sun was a precursor of Lord Rama.[1]

[1]Free Press Journal. 2021. *Ram Navami 2021: Significance, tithi, legend - all you need to know.* [online] Available at: <https://www.freepressjournal.in/india/ram-navami-2021-significance-tithi-legend-all-you-need-to-know> [Accessed 9 October 2021].

CHAPTER EIGHTEEN

Stakes on the Muslim Side

Not much apart from the fact that it was another Masjid from the point of view of Muslims and not as significant as the Mecca-Medina. No doubt the illegal annihilation of the Babri Masjid was not correct and perpetrators should be punished accordingly in a different line of action but to maintain peace the Muslims could have had a masjid elsewhere rather than specifically at the Ram janamBhoomi. From the Right to worship point of view the significance of worship to the Hindus was much more due to that specific location compared to the Muslims. If it is still unclear as to what I mean here then here is an example if God forbid there is some temple is built at the site of Mecca- Medina by breaking down that place and the Hindus demand right to worship there, which party would have the greater right to worship and permission to rebuild? of course, the Muslims because it is their holy revered site. Similar is the case of Ram JanamBhumi, I hope that brings a wave of clarity in the minds of those reading.

CHAPTER NINETEEN

Stakes on the Hindu side

The stakes are heavy on the Hindu side of the things because Ayodhya is the birth place of Shree Ram and not only that but the site of the BabriMasjeed is the true site of the original Ram Mandir as per the 2003 ASI Report which revealed that there were remnants of the original Ram Mandir below the Babrimasjeed hence proving that the Majid was not the original structure at the site and it was built after destroying the original Ram Mandir by the Mughal emperor Babur. Moreover, the importance of Ram Mandir is akin to the importance of Mecca- Medina to the Muslims. Hence any longer denial of the holy site of Hindus to the Hindus could prove to be catastrophe from a peace of mind to the people in general point of view as well as the social, political point of view of the great country that is Bharat or India.

<u>Jurisprudential view of the case</u>

In this case we will take two schools of jurisprudence to analyse the case that is the historical view of jurisprudence and sociological school of jurisprudence.

CHAPTER TWENTY

Historical view of Jurisprudence

This School of thought by the actual name one can accept about the importance it provides for History and it's supporting sources. This School totally centres around the History of the general public, and just through the given history, laws can be made or further changed to create by the general public. Laws are not just for specific gatherings in a general public, rather they are for the whole society, however at that point the inquiry which emerges is that, assuming the law is for the whole society, what will be the source from which laws can be made or taken. That is the reason, history assumes a significant part in this School of thought. At the point when we attempt to comprehend the historical backdrop of a country or a general public, then, at that point, we go over specific practices, customs, convictions which are truth be told followed for a long time and are viewed as holy laws administering that country or the general public. Friedrich Carl Von Savigny is known as the originator of this School of thought. Savigny portrayed law as language since it advances and creates by the immediate powers of religion, customs, propensities and the since long followed traditions continued in a country or society.

Then again, Sir Henry Maine was the organizer and mainproponent of the English historical school of statute. Maine expressed that "The development of reformist social orders has until now been a development from status to contract". This by and large implies that prior there was a proper status of a person without wanting to his/her will however with the advancement of civilisation, presently there is individual opportunity and freedom and everything is the result of the through and through freedom. In the Indian setting, this unrestrained choice isn't outright in nature, as there is a State's sensible limitation on our beloved fundamental rights.

To state in a brief what so far was meant in this School of law is that it underlines on Customs as the wellspring of law for the general public. It's anything but a bunch of rules, rather it changes remembrance over a significant time span at occasion of the general public.

CHAPTER TWENTY-ONE

Sociological School of Jurisprudence

This School of thought was significantly impacted by the Historical School and the legal scholars associated with it. The explanation for it is that both the schools consider society as the premise of law making, both the schools acknowledge the way that there is a specific sort of connection among law and society. This School of thought additionally explained the issues and reactions raised against Historical School as it just thought about customs, religion and convictions of a general public as the wellspring of law, it just took crude sources while taking into account what should be the law for a general public or country. Though, in Sociological School of Jurisprudence, the relationship of a general public with its law and law-production was underscored, expressing those laws will change as per the need of a country or society and this interaction is ever going. This School portrays law as a social marvel and looks at law regarding its effect on a country or society. There are more than four law proponents associated with the advancement of this School, and they are:

- Ihering-He expressed that, " theachievement of law relies on the degree wherein such an equilibrium is accomplished". For his purposes, law never served the singular interests yet rather as a way to the benefit of the general public.

- Ehrlich—According to him, law comprises social realities and doesn't rely upon state authority however relies upon social impulse. He further expresses that the genuine wellspring of law isn't approved laws or points of reference, rather the exercises of society itself.

- Leon Duguit–He presented the term 'Social Solidarity'. Fortitude is only the simple social fact of reliance which joins individuals in a general public and in a country and law ought to be the component to advance or accommodate social fortitude.

Roscoe Pound–He begat the key term still used widely 'Social engineering'. It implies that social architects should help in designing and finding better approaches to forestall social issues through law. He likewise expresses that science of law should look for an improvement of the law as for the general public's need, so the law might do more prominent great.

CHAPTER TWENTY-TWO

Which of the two to choose regarding this verdict or a combination?

There is no straightforward reply to this inquiry on account of the way that this question has its own set of experiences and many individuals have endured and were forfeited during the whole duration of this issue. The way that this is an uncommon situation where two religious networks were slamming into one another over a land parcel, both strict just as human opinions were joined with this debate. Unfortunately, this debate transformed into a communal issue instead of a land debate, that is the reason it is difficult to simply offer a moment response regarding which statute was applied. The way that this judgment was collectively articulated by the Hon'ble seat and the creator is as yet not known, this itself shows how genuine the judgment was to the whole country.

This judgment is absolutely founded on the pertinence of the verifiable proof set by the two sides. Presently, going to the decision and afterward clarifying the law behind it. The Hon'ble Supreme Court of India, was fulfilled and persuaded by the recorded proof and contentions set forth by the Hindu side and the decision was agreeable to them, allowing the Hindu people group to assemble the holy temple and claim the contested land however under the watchful eye of doing as such, the court coordinated that the Central Government will establish a trust who will be dealing with the development of the Temple in Ayodhya. Though, the judgment likewise held that it doesn't legitimize the despoiling and destruction of the Mosque and it expresses that it was contrary to law and order and further offers the Muslim side a piece of 5 ac of land.

As prior expressed the whole judgment depends on verifiable proof, traditions, confidence and convictions. This unquestionably demonstrates that the way of thinking or the statute liked by the Hon'ble court was fairly the Historical school, as just this historical school centres around religion, convictions, customs as a wellspring of law. The proof given by the Hindu side showed restrictive rights over the contested land. The way that the Mosque was before destroyed by the karsevaks and nobody was punished for something very similar, still remaining parts a central issue against the Government and the legal executive with regards to whether hordes are held responsible in such a circumstance. Unmistakably, the destruction of the Mosque is and will consistently be a dim day for our Country's established standards and the rights which our constitution promises us. In the judgment, you'll discover words like, convictions, customs, religion, confidence on various occasions.

This judgment isn't totally founded on the standards of the very expected historical school, rather it has a little touch to the Sociological school, as one can't overlook that the said way of thinking depends on the connection of law with the general public and law changes according to the necessities of the evolving society. This judgment attempted to zero in on something very similar, as before this last decision by the Apex court, different courts since the nineteenth Century, either attempted to resolve the question by preventing the Hindu people group from having any rights over the land and later in the 2010 Allahabad High Court decision, it attempted to oblige both the sides and split the land between the gatherings. We can see that the law in regards to the title of the land was changing right from the principal question.

Henceforth, to gauge which side of the suit had a more grounded guarantee against the contested land, the Hon'ble court depended on the Historical school of law, and to refuse the past decisions, the court has depended on the Sociological school of law.[1]

[1]iPleaders. 2021. *Jurisprudence behind the Ayodhya verdict - iPleaders.* [online] Available at: <https://blog.ipleaders.in/jurisprudence-behind-the-ayodhya-verdict/> [Accessed 9 October 2021].

CHAPTER TWENTY-THREE

Analysis of the historic Ayodhya verdict

This verdict had a massive context in the sense that it dissolved hundreds of years' worth tensions between these two massive communities of the Muslims and the Hindus. This verdict set a new standard of deciding complex disputes that have remained intertwined in the very foundations of the magnificent country that is India and the benchmark for sensitive issue dissolvement was set very high not just in India but around the world. This was a sensitive issue for numerous causes. First it involved literally one of the extremely vitalHindupilgrimage that could be thought of that is the Ram JanmBhumi situated in Uttar Pradesh's prestigious city Ayodhya. Secondly it also involved the matter of destruction of one of the highly disputedBabriMasjeedthat was constructed by the Mughal King Babur in the 16th century. Now this was highly controversial as to on which structure theBabriMasjeed situated on, but it was quite clear as per to the 2003 (Archaeological survey of India) report that concluded that there had beenremainsof a monument that was not a masjid by the assistant sub inspector though not clearly remnants of a Hindu temple. This gave strength to the perceptions regarding Mughals especially to the reign of Babur that he had the habit of destroying pre established temples and building masjids in their place. This was the perception as made in the minds of the judges as well as in the minds of the common people. While the court also didn't in any way justify the demolition of Babri Masjid 1n 1992and termed it against the rule of the law. But let us say that if there was an instance that there was not even an iota of evidence that there was a Ram temple before the Babri Masjid, simply because it is not impossible to completely destroy a structure without leaving its parts beneath the building that is newly built for the reason architectures even in the Mughal period were capable enough but you cannot fight against the religious and customs that have been going from many years. Not just Hindus but even Muslims were of the opinion that the place of contention was Ram Janamsthan and even Muslimsmany witnesses as examined by the courts) referred to it as Babri Masjid built on the Ram Janamsthan. Adding to the fact that "Muslims had not been offering namaz in the particular building from as early as the 1940s.Let's say even if the Muslims had some claim to the property but the truth is that there is no religious significance from the point of view of the Muslims as there is no offering of namaz or any kind of Muslim rituals on the site. Hence this matter was more of a proprietary issue to the Muslims and a right to worship for Hindus. It is a well-established fact that right to property is no longer a fundamental right but a constitutional right under article 300 A.[1] Whereas Freedom of religion falls under article 25-28 of the Indian constitution[2] which also includes the right to worship, it is because One cannot fulfil the obligations of his/her religion without the right to worship unconditionally." If a conflict between them is to happen though of course there would be attempts to harmonise both these rights but it is also for sure that fundamental right will prevail over the legal right in this case however court didn't let the proprietary right get vanquished completely as the honourable court even granted 5 ac (short for acre)at a prominent place in the city of Ayodhya. In such cases it is very key to look at the key picture and not the side factors. It has to be taken into consideration that ram janam Bhoomi had been worshipped since long by the Hindus, on the other hand Muslims had no such claim, let alone they didn't even perform namaz at that place since long. What grave injustice it would have been in terms of fundamental right violation of the Hindu community. Hindus had the full faith, and unconditional devotion to Lord ram while it was no such case for the Muslims. Muslims could easily build there masjid anywhere else in Ayodhya and it would be just another masjid to them but there cannot be another Ram janamBhoomi. Even let us assume that there was a normal namazada(Muslim form of worship) in the babri masjid but the masjid itself is not that important to them as the Ram JanamBhumi to the Hindus. An alternate masjid nearby could be setup and same all routine prayers could have been done and it would make no difference to them. Hence even if there is a clash of two rights of worship hence right to freedom of Religion, we still have to look which side has the superior claim. Ram JanmaBhoomi in this case is like mecca-medina to Muslims, golden temple to Sikhs, St. Peter's Basilica church in Vatican City and I can go on and on. But the point here is the feelings, devotion and strong fundamental rights attached to that place cannot be replicated in any other place and this is the reason why this judgement is significant because it upholds the highest value of the rights that are fundamental rights the spirit to this sacred constitution and the strength of the people of the country. Other factual things include the not giving the entire possession of the land to NirmohiAkhada instead being given a representation in the trust to be formed for temple re building, this was done in order to prevent any sort of possible corruption in the building of the temple because if all reigns are in one party's hands it may lead to questionable decisions, and no one wants that in any case let alone in re building of such an important temple.[3]

[1]2021. [ebook] Available at: <https://legislative.gov.in/sites/default/files/COI_1.pdf> [Accessed 9 October 2021].

[2] ibid

[3]iPleaders. 2021. *Ayodhya Case: India's longest running Dispute - iPleaders*. [online] Available at: <https://blog.ipleaders.in/ayodhya-dispute-case/> [Accessed 9 October 2021].

CHAPTER TWENTY-FOUR

Conclusion

This entire case has been a long, painful, confusing roller coaster ride for the parties involved as well as the people of the country. But the end result has been liberating and refreshing. This judgement has established a very high bench mark for settling complex and sensitive issues. It was really impressive the way supreme court handled all the political, social, media pressure and delivered a judgement based on facts to some extent but most importantly upholding the spirit of right to freedom of religion. This judgement was a proof and a model example for budding lawyers how to overcome pressure situations and rise to the zenith even when no one expects you to have your chins up. Hon'ble Allahabad high court's judgement in 2010 tried to dodge the bullet by dividing the land into three separate parts. But that of course didn't work and only worked as clarified butter(ghee) in this already fired up issue. What followed was social unrest and bereavement of their beloved Shree Ram in the headsof hoi polloi.

But all changed with this remarkable verdict, it took into account several government gazettes during the Britishraajreferring to the Ram JanmBhoomi and even those documents referred the land as Ram janamsthan, further the report of ASI 2003 was deeply analysed and ascertained that there was not at all a mosque there before building the BabriMasjeed and it even sounds illogical from the conquerors that were Mughals point of view why would Babur break one mosque to build another ?when he could have simply chosen another place on the other hand they (especially Babur)[1] was infamous for destroying native infrastructure especially when those belong to worship of other religion.[2] In fact, this is how most "conquerors work, destroy the native place's heritage and religion and force them to follow your own." If truth be told, according to the arguments mentioned by the Hindu side Babri Masjeed hardly looked like a mosque it was not an ideal structure when even looked from an Islamic point of view due to it being made on the ruins of another building.[3]Thus, concluding the fact that there was very less or no significance of Babri Masjid even in form of a worshipping place and more like an ego issue- "we will not tolerate our land being taken". And Supreme Court did the perfect thing even for the Muslim side by gifting 5 ac of land to build a masjid that would be properly built and properly utilized for performing Namaz unlike Babari Masjeed. It's hard to understand any kind of disagreements with this judgement because it is a win-win situation for both the Hindu group and the Muslim group. Babri Masjid was not important to the Muslims like Ram janamsthan was to the Hindus because it was built by a Mughal emperor Babur, he wasn't in any way a religious face in Islam. It can also not be said that witnesses were not given importance aswitnesses almost any person whether Muslim or Hindu were quick to recognise the disputed land as Ram JanamBhumi hence putting a full-fledged final end to this so-called fight which shouldn't have been this way on the very first instance considering the stakes on both sides. But all is well that ends well goes the famous saying and with this I'd like to conclude by saying, Justice was delivered by the five judged bench of this honourable supreme court bench and not denied by any parameter to any side because rights onboth the sides were beautifully contemplated by this bench, no unilateral or one side benefitting decision was given.

[1]Babur, Elliot, H. and Dowson, J., 2006. *Tuzak-i Babari*. Lahore: Sang-e-Meel Publications, pp.272,275.

[2]Hindustanbooks.com. 2021. [online] Available at: <https://www.hindustanbooks.com/pdfs/10120488-Hindu-TemplesWhat-Happend-to-Them-by-Sita-Ram-Goel.pdf> [Accessed 10 October 2021].

[3]Aa.com.tr. 2021. *Babri mosque: Here are key arguments made in court*. [online] Available at: <https://www.aa.com.tr/en/asia-pacific/babri-mosque-here-are-key-arguments-made-in-court/1639873> [Accessed 10 October 2021].

9 798885 306096